Designed and produced by
Aladdin Books Ltd
70 Old Compton Street
London W1

Published in the U.S.A. 1984 by
Gloucester Press
387 Park Avenue South
New York, NY 10016

Insects

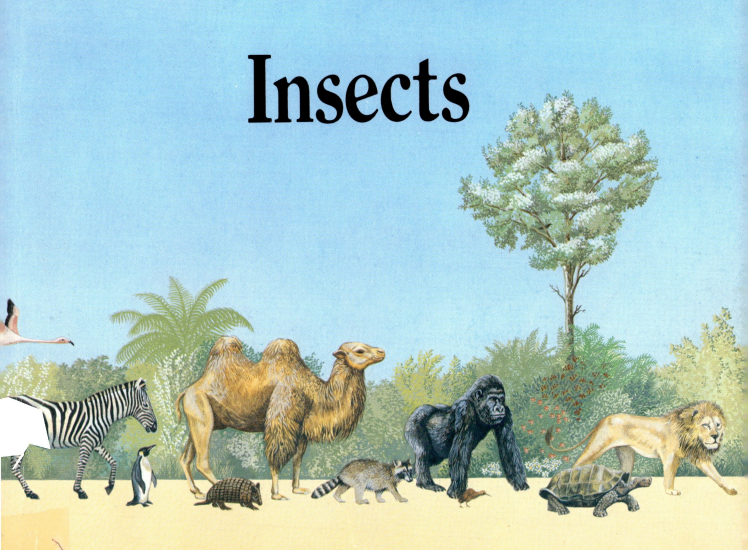

GLOUCESTER PRESS

New York · Toronto · 1984

Art Director   Charles Matheson
Designers   Nick Maddren
                 Pauline Faulks
Editor   Tessa Board

Consultant   Joyce Pope
                 British Museum
                 (Natural History)
                 London

Illustrators   Janet Baker
                   (Maltings Partnership)
                 Peter Barrett
                 Elsa Godfrey
                 Gary Hincks
                 Richard Orr
                 Hugh Schermuly
                 Tony Swift
                 Philip Weare
                 Norman Weaver

*Certain illustrations originally
published in the Closer Look series.*

Contents

Insight

Insects

Casey Horton

What is an insect?

It is fairly easy to tell insects from other types of animals. Even though there is quite a large difference between a stag beetle and a monarch butterfly, virtually all insects have one thing in common making them recognizable as insects; they have three pairs of legs. And, most of them have a body that is divided into three separate parts, or sections.

Insects are arthropods; that is, they are animals which have a body that is enclosed in a hard shell. This shell is the skeleton, and it supports the muscles and protects the soft body underneath. A shrimp is another type of arthropod; when you peel a shrimp, you remove this skeleton.

Insects are not only the largest group of arthropods, they are the largest group of animals, with almost one million different species, or types, alive today. Scientists divide these into 29 smaller groups, or orders. For example, the 75,000 types of true flies belong to the order Diptera.

Grylloblattodea

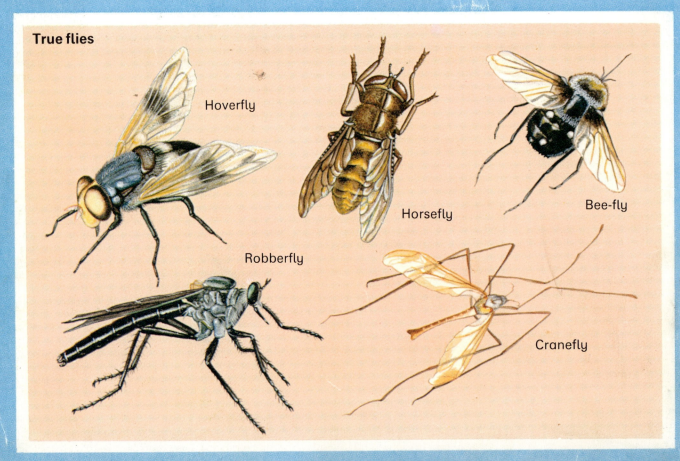

True flies

Hoverfly

Horsefly

Bee-fly

Robberfly

Cranefly

Insect senses

Smelling (antennae)

Feeling (hairs)

Tasting (forelegs)

An insect's eyes

Most insects have three or more eyes, which may be either simple or compound. Simple eyes let in light, but do not form a clear "picture," or image. The compound eye is made up of many small individual eyes – in the dragonfly, each compound eye contains 28,000 smaller eyes! Each individual eye is placed so that it faces in a slightly different direction to the others, and sees only a tiny part of a scene. The brain combines images from each eye. Compound eyes are always in pairs; many insects have a compound eye on each side of their head and several simple eyes arranged above them.

Color vision

Some insects have very good color vision, although the range of colors they see is not the same as the range we see. For example, bees cannot see red; they do see orange, yellow, blue, and violet. In addition, insects such as bees can see colors of ultraviolet light that are invisible to us. Many flowers reflect ultraviolet light. When this happens the insect will not see the color of the flower as we see it. For example, a yellow flower that reflects ultraviolet may appear blue to a bee.

Human and insect color vision

Individual eye

Section through a compound eye

How we see the flower

How the bee may see the flower

Feeding

Larva is the name given to an insect that has not changed into an adult. Larvae are designed for eating and growing; large numbers can easily destroy their food source. Many live on plants and feed on the leaves and stems. Most familiar to us are the caterpillars of moths and butterflies. The swallowtailed moth caterpillar eats ivy, hawthorn and sloe, the puss moth caterpillar lives on willow, and the caterpillar of the small heath butterfly feeds on grasses. Because caterpillars are so abundant they are eaten by birds and other animals, including other insects. Many have disguises such as camouflage, or devices to frighten predators, such as the poisonous taste of the cinnabar and vaporer moth caterpillars, or the fierce-looking "faces" of the puss and elephant hawk moth larvae.

Most caterpillars crawl freely over or inside the plants, but the bagworm moth larva builds a case, or bag around itself as soon as it hatches from the egg. The bag is open at both ends and the larva sticks its head out to gather food.

The large blue butterfly larva begins life quite normally, feeding on the wild thyme, but when it has grown to a certain stage it falls to the ground, where eventually a passing ant may find it. The ant gently strokes the caterpillar, which releases a sweet liquid that ants find very tasty. After some time, the caterpillar hunches its back so that the ant can carry it back to its nest. Once inside, the caterpillar is given ant larvae to eat, and in return it continues to give the ants a sweet milk. The following spring it emerges into the world as a butterfly.

Large blue butterfly and larva with ants

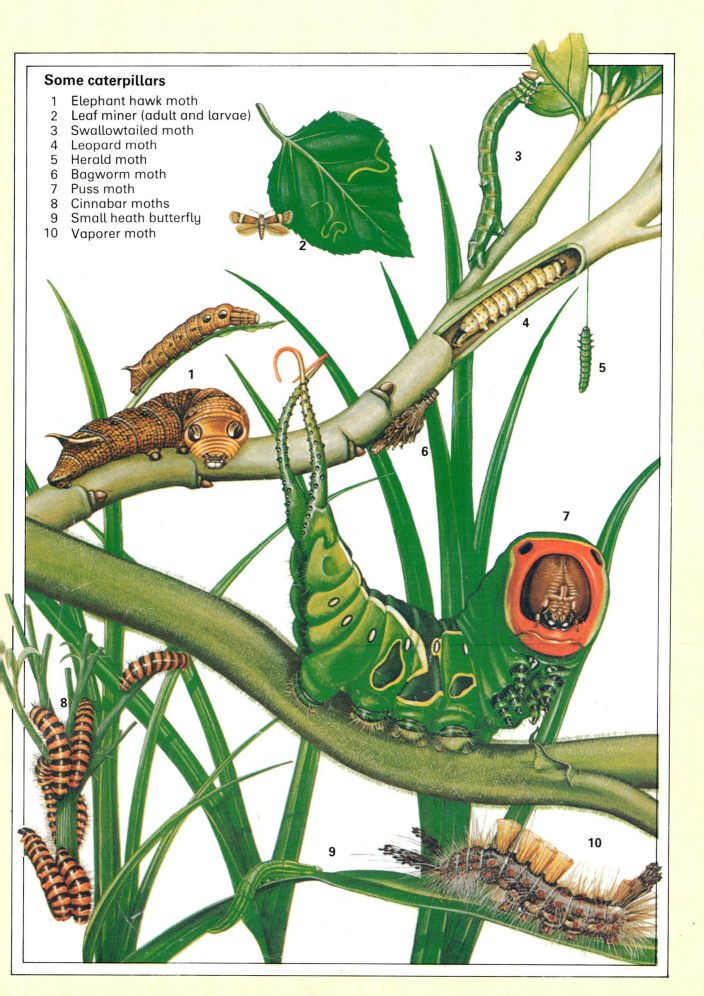

Some caterpillars

1 Elephant hawk moth
2 Leaf miner (adult and larvae)
3 Swallowtailed moth
4 Leopard moth
5 Herald moth
6 Bagworm moth
7 Puss moth
8 Cinnabar moths
9 Small heath butterfly
10 Vaporer moth

Different diets

Insects eat an astounding variety of foods: stems, leaves, flowers, roots, and juices of plants; blood, flesh, hair and fur of animals – as well as whole creatures such as other insects; and plant and animal products such as cloth, wax and flour.

However, insects are also highly specialized eaters. That is, most species are very choosy about what they eat, and only feed on one or two different types of food. The type of food they eat is related to the type of mouth they have, and this is why the insect mouth varies so much from one group of insects to another.

The mouthparts

A typical insect has three pairs of jaws, called the mouthparts. The main pair are the mandibles, which usually have strong "teeth." The second and third pair are the maxillae; the first pair of maxillae may also contain "teeth" and in some insects these jaws are joined together to form a feeding tube called the proboscis. The second pair of maxillae are usually joined together to form the lower lip. An insect's upper lip lies over the main pair of jaws.

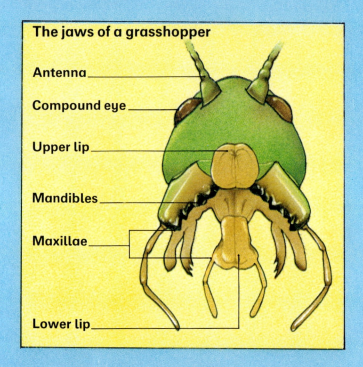

The jaws of a grasshopper

Antenna
Compound eye
Upper lip
Mandibles
Maxillae
Lower lip

The sphinx moth

Most of the butterflies and moths have a proboscis which they use to suck nectar from flowers. The proboscis of the sphinx moth is particularly long, in order to enter the trumpet-like flowers which it visits at night to feed. When this sucking instrument is not in use it coils up under the moth's head.

Sphinx moth feeding

A female mantid devouring its mate

Predators and plant-suckers

Dragonflies, the fastest flying insects, hunt and catch other insects as they both fly through the air. They use their legs to catch and hold their prey and then devour them with their powerful jaws. The mantids also feed on other insects, and in some species the female will even eat the male while he is mating with her! The largest kinds also eat small birds and lizards. Instead of giving chase, they sit quite still with their front legs outstretched and wait for another insect to come within "arms' reach." Both these insects have biting mouthparts.

Insects with piercing mouthparts include blood-sucking female mosquitoes (males feed on nectar) and the plant bugs. Both of these are liquid feeders but they must pierce through tough animal flesh and plant material before they can suck up the fluids. Their long mouthparts are deeply grooved and fit very closely together to make a syringe, which draws up the fluids.

A plant bug feeding

The insect life cycle

Almost every insect begins life as a small egg, which has been laid by the female after she has mated with a male. Insect eggs are usually very small, but they vary in shape. Some have a "lid" on the top through which the larva emerges. Other larvae have to crack the egg case with a "claw" called an egg burster. The egg is the first stage in an insect's life; the larva is the second stage. Ants, bees, butterflies and moths – and some other insects – have two other stages before adulthood. As larvae, they feed continuously until they have outgrown their skeleton, or skin. When this happens, the larva stops feeding and molts: its skin splits and the larva wriggles out.

The final stages

Molting occurs several times. As adults, insects cannot grow because their skeleton is much harder than that of the larva. Therefore, all of an insect's growth must take place while the skeleton is still quite soft. After the final molt, the larva enters its third stage and starts to pupate. That is, it makes a cocoon around itself which hides it from the outside world. Inside the cocoon, the insect (now called a pupa, or chrysalis) undergoes a very dramatic change. Its body tissues are broken down and then re-formed into an adult body. This change is called metamorphosis. Finally, the adult emerges from the cocoon and begins the fourth stage of its life cycle. This type of life cycle is called complete metamorphosis.

Monarch butterfly laying eggs

Larva emerging from its egg case

Robin moth in flight

Growing caterpillar and pupa of a swallowtail butterfly

Robin moth emerging from the cocoon

15

Growing bigger

Insects that only go through three stages of growth and change (called incomplete metamorphosis) include the grasshoppers and dragonflies. When the larva hatches from the egg case it looks like a small wingless version of the adult, and is called a nymph. The nymph goes through several phases of eating, growing, resting and then molting. After the final molt the full-grown winged adult emerges from the old skin.

Nearly all dragonfly females lay their eggs in the water, although some deposit them on the stems of water plants. The larvae live in water, either among the weeds of a river or pond, or on the muddy bed. They are equipped with very sharp jaws which act like pincers, and they feed on small fish or other water creatures.

Many nymphs feed for two years before their final molt. They then climb from the water onto a plant stem. Their skin splits along the back and the beautiful winged adult flies off in search of food.

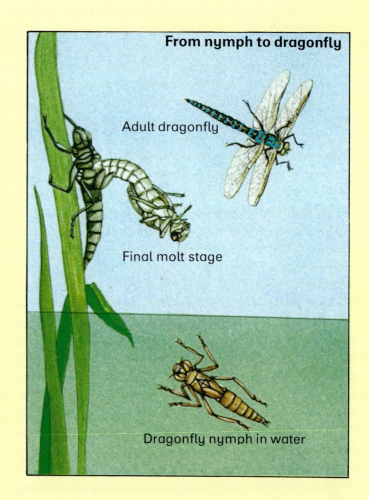

From nymph to dragonfly

Adult dragonfly

Final molt stage

Dragonfly nymph in water

The final molt of a grasshopper

The three previous nymph stages

Female aphids being born live

Life in a clay pot

The female potter wasp makes a number of nests out of wet mud which dry to a hard clay. The nest may be built on the ground, in which case it looks exactly like a vase with a wide mouth; or it may resemble a small clay pot which the wasp fastens to a plant stem, usually some way from the ground. After making the nests the wasp goes in search of other insects' larvae such as caterpillars, which she paralyzes with her sting. The prey is then taken to the nest and placed inside. The wasp continues to hunt until the nest is almost full. She then lays a single egg in it.

Once the egg has hatched the wasp larva feeds on the caterpillars, which are still alive. Usually, by the time the wasp larva has eaten all the food it is ready to pupate. When the new adult emerges from the cocoon it cracks the clay and is free to fly away. Adult potter wasps feed on nectar and sap.

Potter wasp building a nest

Breeding without mating

Aphids have two distinct ways of breeding. Males and females mate in the fall, and the females lay their eggs on leaves. The parents then die, but the eggs remain where they are until the spring, when they hatch into females.

These females then produce more females. Aphids are one of a few types of insect which are able to breed without first mating with a male. When the population is large enough, *winged* females fly off to start new colonies of females on other plants.

The young hatch inside the female's body and are born live. They are able to breed in the same way within eight to ten days. It is because aphids breed so rapidly during the summer that they are such pests in gardens and on farms. In the fall winged males and winged females are produced. They mate and then die after the females have laid their eggs.

Insect defenses

Animals that spend most of their time in the open must have some way of protecting themselves against predators. Insects rely very much on disguise to hide from birds and other insect-eaters. The peppered moths, for example, live among trees, and their wings are colored or patterned in such a way that the moths are almost invisible when they rest on lichen-covered bark. In areas where air pollution is high, and tree trunks and buildings have been blackened with soot, the moth is black.

Other mimics

The stick and leaf insects, and some tropical leaf butterflies, such as the kallima, are also very good at hiding while remaining in the open. They actually mimic parts of the plants they live on. As stick insects stay still much of the time it is difficult to tell the insect from the stem. The same is true of the leaf insects and butterflies. The moving leaf insect lives and feeds on leaves and its body is shaped and colored like one. This disguise is so good that other insects that eat leaves often try to bite it!

Poisonous insects

Heliconid butterfly

Burnet moth

Tiger moth

Beware! dangerous insects

The bright and attractive colors of many insects warn predators that the insect is dangerous; it may just taste nasty, it may sting, or be poisonous. Warning colors are red, black and white, or black and yellow. Many moths and butterflies contain substances which bring death if eaten in large quantities. Usually, once an animal has tasted one, it avoids eating others.

The moving leaf insect

A tropical leaf butterfly — Kallima

Butterfly in flight

Butterfly at rest

Peppered moths

The element of surprise

Another type of insect defense is found in many winged insects such as some moths and mantids. In these insects the upperside of the wing has a large, round, bold pattern that looks very much like an eye, and is known as an "eyespot." When these insects are disturbed or provoked they will suddenly flash their wings. This generally has the effect of startling the intruder which may be frightened or confused enough to be driven away.

Eyespots on a moth

Communication

Insects use colors and patterns to communicate with other animals, but many insects are also able to pass messages to members of their own species. Nearly all the butterflies and moths, for example, use scent to show that they are ready to breed.

Those insects that live together and rely on each other for finding and gathering food and building a nest, have developed very complex ways of communicating.

Ants and termites produce special substances in their body which they pass on to other members in the nest. These substances are chemicals called pheromones. Each type of pheromone triggers off a certain activity in the insect that receives the message. That is, it "tells" the insect what to do. Ants exchange pheromones in their saliva when they feed or lick each other.

Bee language

Honeybees produce a strong smelling pheromone in their abdomen. One of its uses is to guide lost bees back to the hive. Once a bee has searched for and found the hive it rests on the outside with its abdomen pointing outwards. The bee then fans its wings, wafting the scent through the air so other bees follow it home.

These bees also perform dances to tell members of the hive where to look for nectar. The simplest is the round dance; it tells the bees to look for food within a short distance of the hive, and is performed by running in a circle, first one way and then the other. The waggle dance is more complex. It is done in a figure eight, with a long run down the middle. It not only tells the others the distance of flowers from the hive, but also in which direction the bees should fly to reach them.

The ant "kiss"

A Brazilian firebug (firefly)

Fireflies

Fireflies are found in tropical areas, and in cooler regions in southern Europe and North America (where they are often called lightning bugs). These beetles may give off a green, red or yellow light, and one species actually produces all three colors, like a traffic light. The light is produced in a special organ on the underside of the abdomen. Both male and female fireflies are able to "light up."

Some female fireflies will gather in large numbers in a tree, making a very spectacular display. In some parts of South America and the West Indies, people catch fireflies and place them in a lantern, or in their hair, to light their way in the dark, or even to wear as brooches!

Light and sound

Butterflies and moths are not the only insects that communicate to the opposite sex before they mate. Some insects can produce either light or sound with which they let the world know that they are looking for a mate. Crickets, cicadas and grasshoppers use sound to attract mates; fireflies and glow-worms use light.

Crickets

Male crickets and grasshoppers signal their readiness to mate by "singing," or stridulating. Crickets sit on the ground and sing to the females, which fly about above them. The song is not really a song, but the sound made when one front wing rubs against the other.

A toothed vein on the right wing acts like a file and this rubs against a small area on the left wing, called the scraper. The scraper acts as a resonator; that is, it makes the sound louder.

A male cricket stridulating

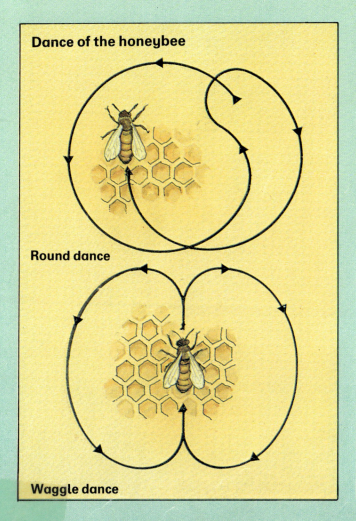

Dance of the honeybee

Round dance

Waggle dance

Bees and wasps

Insects that live and work together in groups are called social insects. Examples are the honeybees, bumblebees, the common wasp, and its North American relative, the yellowjacket. Social bees make a nest, or hive, from wax that is made in special glands on their body. The hive of wild honeybees is often in a hollow tree.

Members of the hive are divided into castes, or classes: workers, drones and a queen. The queen is in charge of the colony and produces all the eggs after she has mated with a drone (male bee).

Workers are female bees that cannot lay eggs; they do what their name suggests – they work. They gather nectar and pollen, build and repair the nest and take care of the queen, eggs and larvae. Honeybees are the only bees that build a permanent nest in which the colony survives from one year to the next.

Social wasps

In common wasps and yellowjackets, the queen is the only member of the wasp nest that lives through the winter. In the spring she emerges from hibernation to build a new nest.

This is usually built in the ground and is made of paper which the queen produces by chewing pieces of wood and mixing this with her saliva to make a pulp. She starts to build by hanging a pillar from a support. Out from this she builds a curved "ceiling" from which she hangs a number of cells.

One egg is laid in each cell; when the larvae hatch the queen feeds them until they become adult workers. In late summer, male wasps are produced, together with females that are capable of laying eggs. These females are future queens that will mate with the males before leaving the nest in the fall.

Underground wasp nest

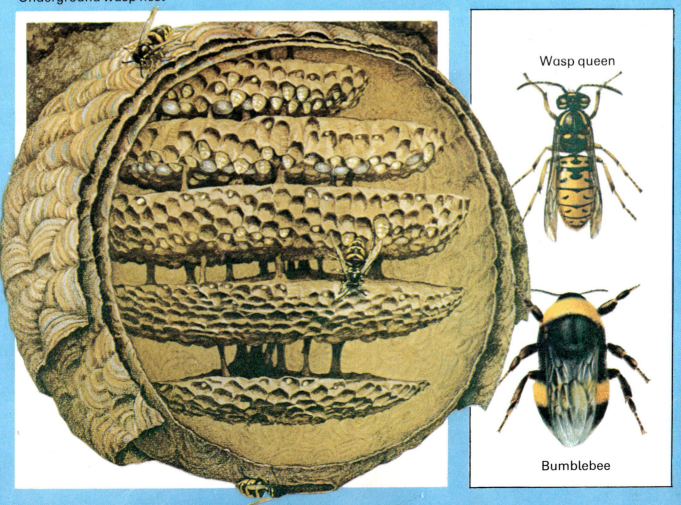
Wasp queen

Bumblebee

Ants and termites

The two other social insects are the ants and termites. Although they are quite similar in appearance and habits, they are not closely related. Ants belong to the same group as the bees and wasps, and termites make up a group of their own.

Unlike bees and wasps, all ants and termites are social insects; none of them live on their own.

Ant larvae pupate before becoming adults; in the termites the larvae are miniature versions of adults.

Termite hills

Most termites build hard nests, or hills, from their droppings. Some species build mound-like structures that are about 120 cm (2 ft) across; but there are termites in Africa and Australia that build hills three times the height of a man. These huge towers may contain up to two million insects. Other types of nests include those made underground and those that are built, like wasps' nests, from wood that is chewed to make paper.

Most termites live in tropical areas of the world but a few species are found in southern Europe and America.

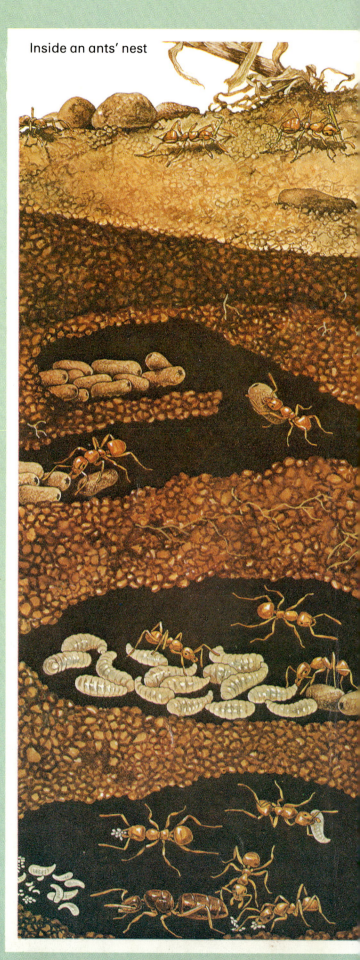
Inside an ants' nest

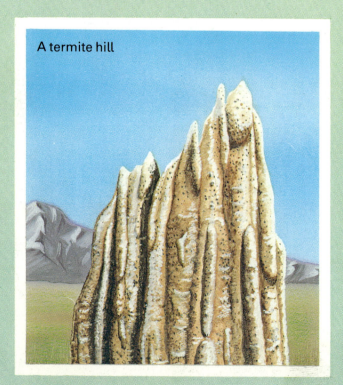
A termite hill

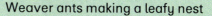
Weaver ants making a leafy nest

Ant nests

Most ants make their nest underground. The nest is a series of tunnels leading to a number of chambers, including a room for the queen, which lays all the eggs, and rooms which are used as nurseries. In many ant colonies soldier ants guard the nest against intruders and special workers called scouts, go in search of food. Ants usually mate once a year, when males and females grow wings and fly the nest. After mating the male dies and the female begins a new colony.

The weaver ants are one of several species that make their nests on plants. Workers pull overlapping leaves together by standing in a row along the edge of one leaf and reaching up to grab the edge of the second leaf in their jaws. Other workers now appear carrying larvae in their mouth, which they pass back and forth along the joints where the two leaves meet. The larvae produce a sticky silk thread which binds the leaves together into a bag.

Beetles

The beetles make up the largest group of insects, with about 300,000 species. A typical beetle has two pairs of wings, although only the hind wings are used in flying. The forewings are hard and cover the hind wings and abdomen. When the beetle flies, it holds its forewings apart.

Beetles great and small

Many beetles are carnivores or scavengers, feeding on living or dead animals; others, such as weevils and chafers, feed on plants.

Weevils are often wingless, or if they do have wings, fly very little. All have a long snout which they use to pierce holes in plants. The female nut weevil, for example, drills a hole in a hazelnut in which she lays an egg. In America, the cotton boll weevil lays its eggs in the buds of the cotton plant, causing considerable damage to cotton crops.

The great diving beetle is an aggressive insect that lives in water. Both larvae and adults feed on small fish and tadpoles, and sometimes on other water beetle larvae. The rove beetles are mostly small in size with small wings that do not cover their long abdomen, but they fly well and can run fast. These beetles feed on other insects or on decaying vegetation. The lamellicorn beetle, despite its fearsome appearance, is a plant-feeder.

Living on waste

Dung beetles are found in all parts of the world except Antarctica. They are compact, rather attractive creatures with interesting habits. They get their name from the fact that they feed on animal droppings, or dung.

When the female is ready to lay her eggs, she and the male make a ball of dung and roll it into a hole in the ground, where they bury it. Now the female makes the ball into a pear shape, and lays an egg at the narrower end. The larva feeds on the dung until it has hollowed out the inside. After the larva has pupated, the adult crawls out and makes its way to the surface.

The burying, or sexton beetles of Europe have a similar life cycle, although they feed on dead animals. In this case the male and female bury a small animal such as a mouse, and the female chews the flesh into a ball. She lays her eggs in nearby tunnels so that the developed larvae can feed on the flesh.

Great diving beetles

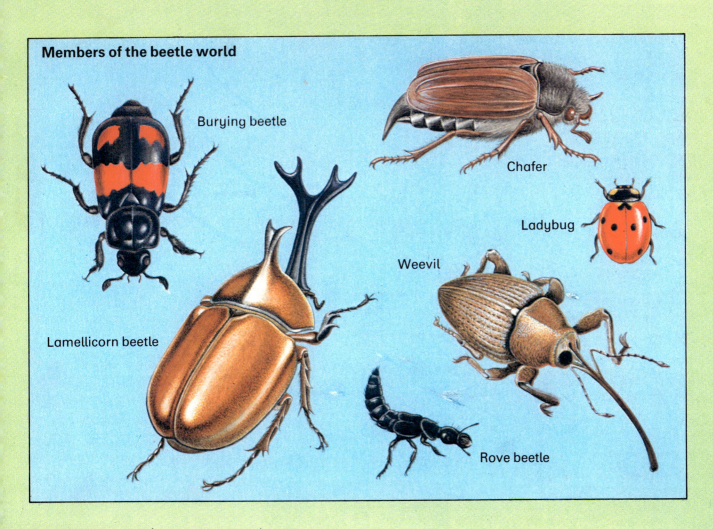

Members of the beetle world

Burying beetle

Chafer

Ladybug

Weevil

Lamellicorn beetle

Rove beetle

Dung beetles preparing a nest

Bugs

In North America, the word "bug" is sometimes used for any insect or creepy crawler. But the true bugs make up one group of insects, all of which have piercing and biting mouthparts in the shape of a beak. This is one way of telling them from beetles, most of which have biting mouthparts. And all bugs have incomplete metamorphosis, whereas in beetles it is complete.

Carnivorous land bugs include the assassin bug and the leaf-footed bug. The assassin bug has a powerful, curved beak and strong forelegs with which it grabs its prey. These insects feed by external digestion. Once they have a firm grip on their victim, they pierce it with the beak.

A poisonous digestive juice flows down from the insect's mouth, into the victim's body. These juices quickly dissolve the tissues inside, and the liquid food is then sucked up into the insect's mouth.

Water bugs

The water bugs are found mainly in the still or slow-moving waters of ponds, lakes and ditches. The pond skaters and water crickets are adapted for living on the surface. Pond skaters have very short front legs with which they catch prey such as gnats. The other two pairs of legs are used for moving about; the middle pair are used like oars, and the back pair for steering.

The water boatman or backswimmer uses its long hind legs to propel itself, upside-down. Its food includes insect larvae and tadpoles, which it feeds on in the same way as the assassin bug. In Australia the backswimmer is called a "toe biter" because it can pierce human flesh with its beak. The water scorpion also stings with its beak; its "tail" is a breathing tube. Many water bugs can fly when they are out of the water, but the saucer bug cannot; it walks from pond to pond.

Pond dwellers

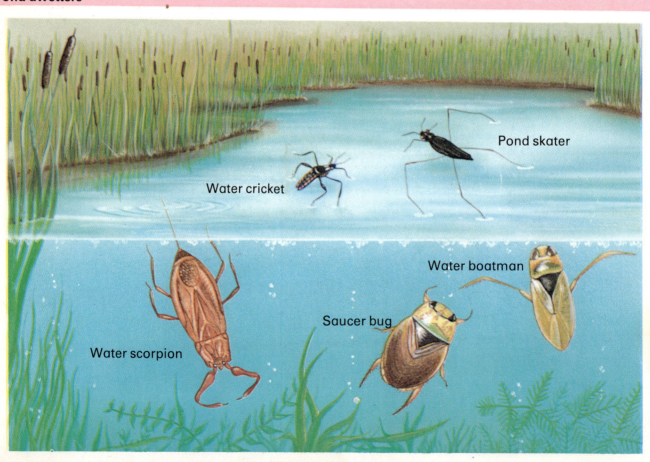

Pond skater

Water cricket

Water boatman

Saucer bug

Water scorpion

Shieldbugs

All of the shieldbugs have flattened bodies, and in most the back is shaped like a shield which gives these insects their name. Like the beetles they have two pairs of wings but only use the hind wings for flying. In America some shieldbugs have been given the name stinkbug; this is because they give off a very powerful, foul-smelling liquid when they are threatened.

Most shieldbugs live in warm climates, and all of them live on trees, shrubs or herbs. Some of them restrict themselves to certain plants; for example the green shieldbug lives on hazel and birch trees, while the pied shieldbug is found on white dead-nettle. Eggs may be laid either on the plant or on the ground.

The pied shieldbug lays eggs on the soil, and when the nymphs have emerged from the eggs, the female leads them to the food plant where they will feed as adults.

Green shieldbug

Brassica bug

Pied shieldbug

Shieldbugs

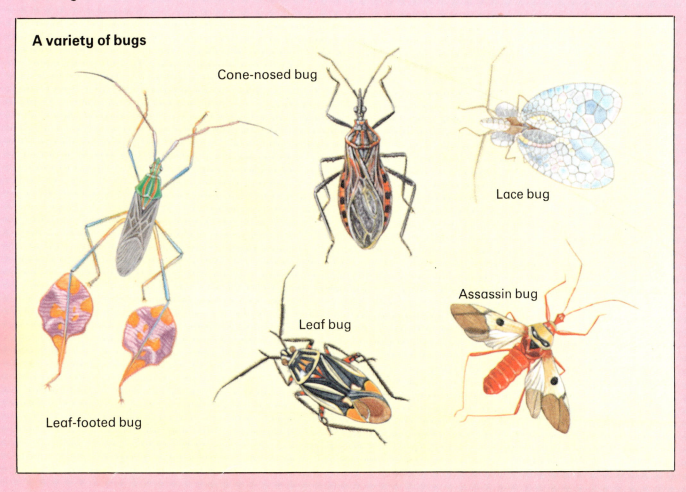

A variety of bugs

Cone-nosed bug

Lace bug

Leaf bug

Assassin bug

Leaf-footed bug

Butterflies and moths

Butterflies and moths belong to the same order of insects, in which there are some 165,000 different species. The majority of these are moths. It is sometimes difficult to tell a moth from a butterfly, for some of the moths are as brightly colored as the butterflies, and also fly about during the day. As a general rule, however, it is the butterflies that appear in the day and the moths that come out at night.

Other differences are that butterflies have "knobs" on the ends of their antennae and they usually fold their wings in an upright position when they rest. Moths normally fold their wings flat, the forewings over the hindwings.

Most butterflies and moths live in the tropics, although they are, of course, also found in cooler regions of the world during the summer months. As a group, the adults feed exclusively on the nectar they take from flowers. Some, however, do not feed at all as adults. The emperor moth is one example.

Long distance flying

In the insect world there are often species that undertake long journeys from one country to another. Examples are the monarch, or milkweed butterfly, and some of the hawk moths. The monarch butterfly of North America spends the summer in the northern regions of the U.S. and the southern regions of Canada. In the fall these butterflies migrate in large numbers, flying as far south as Florida and Mexico.

During their flight they come to rest at night in trees, and once they have reached their destination they go into semi-hibernation, flying about only now and then from their perches among the trees. On the return flight, the females lay their eggs; this time the butterflies usually make their way back more or less on their own.

The hawk moths are fast flying insects. The convolvulus hawk moth breeds in Africa and from there makes its way northwards, flying across the Alps and appearing in Great Britain in late summer.

Eyed hawk moth feeding at night

Some European butterflies

1 Purple hairstreak
2 Large tortoiseshell
3 Black hairstreak
4 Marsh fritillary
5 Gatekeeper
6 Orange tip
7 Peacock
8 Checkered skipper

Insect pests

Insect pests fall into two groups: those that affect plants and those that affect animals. The European cabbage butterfly is frequently seen fluttering about the garden, alighting on nasturtiums and brassicas (such as cabbage and broccoli).

These butterflies lay their eggs on the leaves, where the caterpillars will feed. The codlin moth lays its eggs on fruits trees, such as apple, and the caterpillars crawl inside the apple and feed until they are ready to pupate.

Swarms of migratory locusts can cause famines when they devour crops. Pests that cause damage to plants in both Europe and America include the colorado (potato) beetle and the bark beetles. One species of bark beetle spreads Dutch elm disease; as it tunnels beneath the bark it spreads a fungus through the tree. It is the fungus that actually causes the disease which ends up killing the elm, not the beetle.

European cabbage butterfly, adult and larva

Codlin moth, adult and larva

The results of Dutch elm disease

Bark beetle

Pests that affect animals

Fleas are found in most parts of the world, and feed mainly on the blood of mammals and birds. Although for the most part they usually only cause an irritating bite, fleas that live on rats have been responsible for spreading plagues. They spread disease through a bacterium that is carried in their saliva. Flies also spread disease.

Mosquitoes spread malaria and yellow fever; houseflies, bluebottles and greenbottles can cause gastric diseases where there is poor hygiene. The tsetse fly of Africa causes the deadly sleeping sickness in humans and also a disease that affects cattle and horses.

The common housefly feeds on decaying food and dead animals. When it lands on something, it tastes it with its feet, and if it is edible, automatically begins to feed with its proboscis. Because it lives on rotting matter it picks up bacteria, which then spread to whatever food it lands on next.

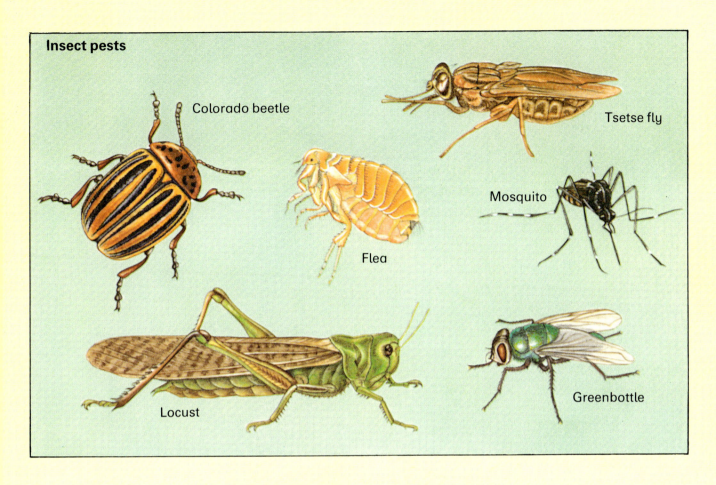

Insect pests

Colorado beetle

Tsetse fly

Flea

Mosquito

Locust

Greenbottle

The cottony cushion scale

Scale insects generally damage plants, but the cottony cushion scale was responsible for the death of several hundred thousand orange trees in California in the late 1800s. This insect originated in Australia and was accidentally introduced to America in 1868. The adults live on the stems or leaves of citrus trees, sucking the sap. Once the larvae have hatched they creep about to find a suitable place to feed. When they are settled, a protective waxy substance develops within the skin, giving the larvae their "scaly" appearance.

The adult females lay eggs without mating. The eggs are laid under the scale and deposited in a mass of fibers that look like cotton wool, although it is in fact wax.

The pest was only brought under control when an Australian species of ladybug, the scale insect's natural enemy, was brought to California. This type of pest control is known as biological control.

Cottony cushion scales and their predators

Amazing insects

Insects come in so many shapes and sizes, and have such interesting habits, that it could be said that most of them are amazing in some way. Just two examples are the stick insect and leaf-footed bug. The rather unimpressive stick insect has a remarkable ability to grow new legs and antennae. If one of these is damaged or falls off, a new one grows in its place.

And the spiny leaf-footed bug has a fascinating way of caring for its eggs. The female sticks them on to the male's back, which is covered in spines, so the eggs are very well protected.

However, there are some insects that are amazing because they have some particularly dramatic shape or pattern on part of their body.

Long beetle and lantern fly
The long beetle is very closely related to the weevil. Like the weevil it has a beak, but in this case the beak is exceptionally long – almost as long as the body.

The antennae are also very long, and as this beetle is almost blind, it depends on its antennae for finding its way and its food. The long beetle bores holes in wood, fruit and sometimes in ant or termite nests.

Many species of lantern flies have odd, almost monstrous heads. But one species is even more peculiar than the others, with its huge hollow growth. The patterns on the head look like teeth, eyes and a horn, but they are just patterns. They are probably useful for frightening birds and other predators.

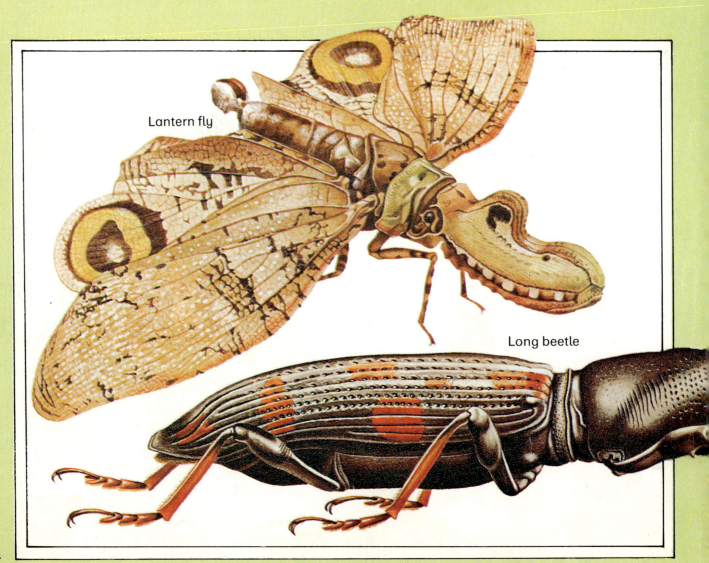

Lantern fly

Long beetle

The incredible treehoppers

A group of insects that are related to the cicada and aphid are known as hoppers. They include planthoppers, and one of the most common is the froghopper. The froghopper larva is the insect that makes the frothy mass of foam on plants which is called cuckoo spit. While the planthoppers have a quite remarkable appearance, they are outdone by the treehoppers.

These insects look so spectacular that they are almost unbelievable. In the small treehoppers the skeleton at the front of the thorax is enlarged and has a fantastic shape. For example, the buffalo treehopper is shaped like a buffalo head, with two horns on the top. Other treehoppers have shapes that resemble thorns, flowers and other parts of plants.

Scientists once thought that a treehopper's appearance was used to hide it among plants, but as some of these insects are found on plants which they do not resemble, this is not always true.

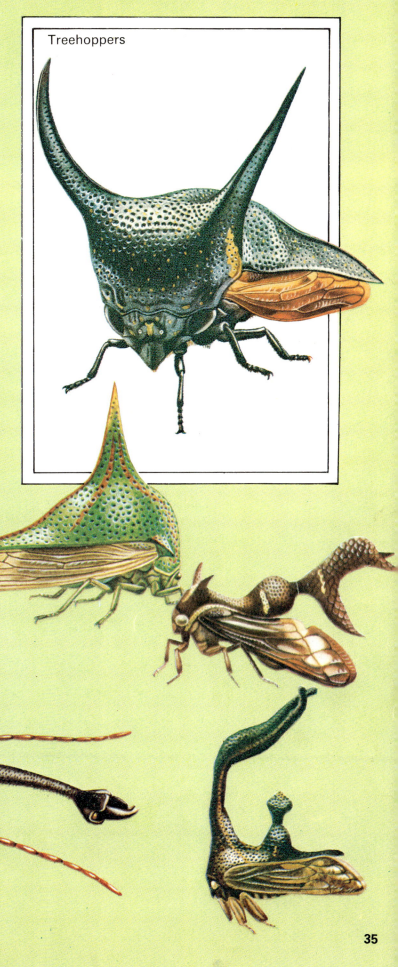

Treehoppers

Glossary

Antennae
Pair of structures on an insect's head, sometimes called feelers. They are used for touching, smelling and tasting.

Arthropods
A large group of animals that have a hard skeleton (exoskeleton) on the outside of the body. They include spiders, insects, and crustaceans such as lobsters, crabs and shrimp.

Carnivorous
Used to describe any animal that feeds on animal flesh.

Larvae
Name given to insects that have hatched from the egg but have not yet become adults. The caterpillar is an example. (Larva is the singular form.)

Mandibles
The first and major pair of an insect's jaws.

Maxillae
The second and third pairs of jaws.

Metamorphosis
A word used to describe the change from young insect to adult.

Nymph
Like larva, a young insect between the egg and adult stage. It is used for insects that have incomplete metamorphosis, such as the dragonflies.

Ovipositor
A long thin tube at the end of a female's abdomen. It is used to lay eggs but in some insects has evolved into a sting.

Predator
An animal that hunts and eats other animals.

Proboscis
A long tube formed from an insect's mouthparts that is used to suck nectar from flowers.

Pupae
Insects undergoing metamorphosis within the cocoon. Sometimes called chrysalides. (Pupa is the singular form.)

Social insect
An insect that lives and co-operates with other insects of the same species.

Solitary insect
An insect that lives entirely on its own and only comes together with another during mating.

Index